Costa Rica

When Woman Became the Sea

A Costa Rican Creation Myth

Written by
Susan Strauss

Illustrated by
Cristina Acosta

BEYOND
WORDS
Publishing
I N C

To my daughter Isabella,
who taught me
to paint like a child.
With love,

— Cristina —

For my daughter,
Geneva Latisse-Laura,
who loves to drink clean,
sweet, fresh water.
May the waters she drinks
all of her life be sweet.

— Susan —

Beyond Words Publishing, Inc.

20827 N.W. Cornell Road, Suite 500 • Hillsboro, Oregon 97124-9808

503-531-8700 / 1-800-284-9673

Text copyright © 1998 by Susan Strauss
Illustrations copyright © 1998 by Cristina Acosta

Edited by Michelle Roehm
Designed by DesignWise

Distributed to the book trade by Publishers Group West
Printed in Italy

LIBRARY OF CONGRESS CATALOGING-IN-PUBLICATION DATA

Strauss, Susan.
　　When woman became the sea : a Costa Rican creation myth / adapted
by Susan Strauss ; illustrated by Cristina Acosta.
　　　　p. cm.
　　Summary: Sibu creates a woman to be the wife of Thunder but when she
asserts her independence from both of them, a spectacular tree and all the beautiful
waters of the world spring forth from her.
　　ISBN 1-885223-85-4
　　[1. Folklore—Costa Rica. 2. Creation—folklore. 3. Ocean—
Folklore.] I. Acosta, Cristina, ill. II. Title.
PZ8.1.S893Wh 1998
398.2'097286'01—dc21
　　　　　　　　　　　　　　　　　　　　　　　　　　　　98-17470
　　　　　　　　　　　　　　　　　　　　　　　　　　　　CIP
　　　　　　　　　　　　　　　　　　　　　　　　　　　　AC

Finding the Science in the Myth

This creation story comes from the Cabecar and Bribri people of Costa Rica and reveals two great miracles of our planet. One is the tree. The other is water. It is fitting that Costa Rica brings us a creation story about trees and water, since that country hosts one of the world's largest rain forests, which they call the Cloud Forest because thick clouds are always dancing between the jungle trees.

Trees and water work their miracles day and night. Without them, life on earth would not exist. Water nourishes our planet as it travels through the soil, plants, and air. Water cleans and purifies itself as it soaks down through layers of soil and rock after a rainstorm. Eventually, through streams and rivers that flow both underground and overland, rainwater finds its way to the sea.

Trees are vitally important to this cycle of water. After it rains, trees soak up enormous quantities of water through their roots. The water travels up the trunk of the tree, out to the branches, and then evaporates through the leaves.[1] This releases the water back into the atmosphere to form clouds again. On a warm day, thousands of gallons of water evaporate from a *single* acre of forest. Trees store the largest amount of water where their trunks meet the ground. This "belly" of the tree is called the *bole*,[2] which sounds very much like the Spanish word for tree, *árbol*.

Since trees are great storage places for water and help cycle water back into the atmosphere, their presence increases rainfall in an area. More rain and water attracts more birds and animals, who can make their homes in the trees. For these reasons, trees are often depicted as mothers in the myths of the world.

And the father? Is there a father of water? In the long-ago time when the earth was first forming, large bodies of gases flowed around the earth's atmosphere. At times, electrical storms brewed up shocks of lightning and thunder. Gases like oxygen and hydrogen were content to ignore each other, but when pierced by electric bolts of lightning, the two gases bonded. This bond, or "marriage," was so strong that the "child" of this marriage was not a gas at all—and water was born! So, in the special language of myth, the tree is the mother and lightning/thunder is the father of water.

Some think that ancient peoples created myths because they didn't have science to explain the world. As you will discover in this tale, myths are actually poetic images of science. Some early peoples observed nature with the same keen perception achieved by modern scientists. They preserved their observations in sacred stories that we now call myths.

1. Technically, scientists call this *transpiration*.
2. *Bole* is a term used by tree scientists, who are called *silviculturists*.

In the long-ago time,
Sibu was creating the world.
Sibu was making all manner
of mountains ... and jungles ... and
valleys deep and low. Sibu created
all kinds of creatures—creeping,
crawling ones ... running, jumping
ones ... and soaring, flying ones.

But wait—something was missing!

"What is it?
What is missing?"

Sibu asked himself.

But he couldn't figure it out.

Sometimes even the creator needs a little help being creative. So, Sibu called for his friend Thunder. (He always had an electric idea.) "THUNDERRRRRRRRRR!"

But Thunder was busy dancing across the sky. KKKKKIPPPU He would be here one moment, and the next— KKKKKIPPPUUUMMM!

he was gone.

So, Sibu called again, "THUNDERRRRRRRRR!"
But Thunder enjoyed his sky dancing, and he paid no attention.

Sibu decided that he had to create something— something so dazzling ... so magnificent ... so exquisite ... so that he could catch Thunder's attention and hold it. It had to be something so beautiful ... so sensitive ... so mesmerizing ... so ...

So, Sibu created the first woman.

Her name was

Sea.

She was enchanting.
Her hair was as black
as the night, her skin
was brown and warm
like the earth, and her eyes
sparkled like the stars.

The moment Thunder caught sight of her—

KKKKKIPPPUUUMMM!

he was there, right next to her. He asked her
to be his wife. Sea agreed, and soon
she became full with child.

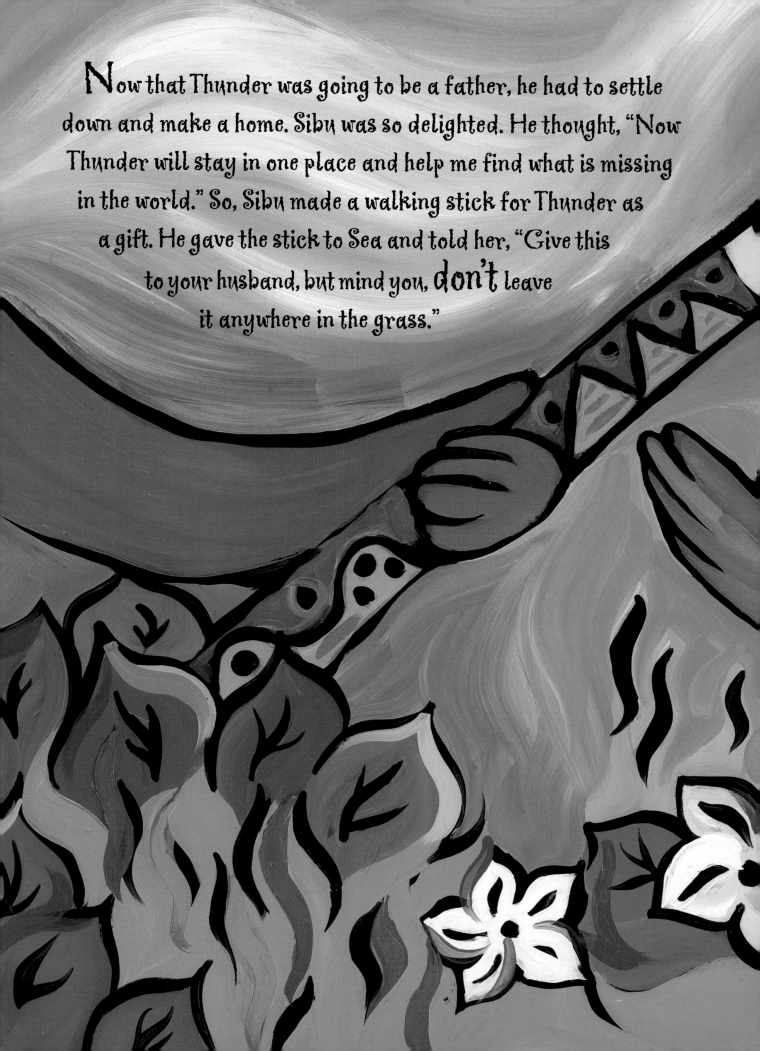

Now that Thunder was going to be a father, he had to settle down and make a home. Sibu was so delighted. He thought, "Now Thunder will stay in one place and help me find what is missing in the world." So, Sibu made a walking stick for Thunder as a gift. He gave the stick to Sea and told her, "Give this to your husband, but mind you, **don't** leave it anywhere in the grass."

Sea took the walking stick and traveled over mountains and valleys ... and more mountains and more valleys ... until she arrived home.

When she gave the walking stick to Thunder, he was

FURIOUS!

"What?" he stormed, "Does he think I, Thunder, am some old man? Does he think that I, Thunder, need a walking stick to get around? **Take it back to Sibu!** But mind you, **don't** leave it anywhere in the grass."

So, Sea took the walking stick and traveled back over mountains and valleys ... and more mountains and more valleys ... until

she began to wonder.

"I wonder why I have to listen to this one man telling me to do one thing and I wonder why I have to listen to this other man telling me to do something else? And I wonder why I can't just leave this stick here in the grass?"

And so she did.

For the next time Sea came
walking through that valley,
there was a snake in the grass,
and
it bit her.

She slipped into such a strange sleep that it seemed she was dead.

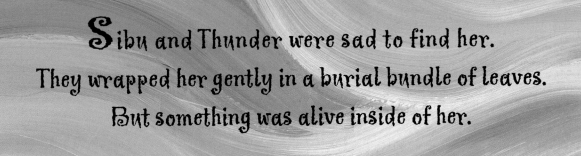

Sibu and Thunder were sad to find her.
They wrapped her gently in a burial bundle of leaves.
But something was alive inside of her.

All at once, the bundle began
to bulge and balloon and bounce
off the ground.

Sibu grabbed a frog,
put him on the bundle, and said,
"There, hold this bundle down and stay in one place!"

Oh, how the world is changed by creatures who can't stay in one place!

For the first fly that flew by
caught the frog's eye, and he was off hopping after it.

Now, the bundle once again began to
bounce and bounce and bulge and balloon,
until all at once it BURST open!
A magnificent tree sprouted forth from inside.

The tree stretched and pushed, climbing high into the sky.
It stretched a branch high and far in one direction.
It stretched another branch high and far
in the other direction.

This woman named Sea
was now a spectacular tree!

Leaves and blossoms burst out.
Birds of every color, birds of every feather,
came to rest and make their nests in this tree.
Oh! There was such a lot of
Caaa,
Caaa, Cahrr, Cahrr,
cacophony of calls echoing between the leaves.
This caught the attention of Sibu, who cried,

"What is all that
racket down there?"

When he saw the tree piercing up through the heavens, he called his two favorite birds, Tijerita, the scissor-tailed flycatcher, and Pajarillo d'Aqua, the grebe. They flew to the top of the great tree and pulled it down, down, down, down, down until the tree began to

CRRRRAACKKK!

and the great belly of the tree BURST open. All the waters of the world flowed forth from the belly of the tree and filled in the lands around the mountains, making shores and distant shores.

Branches that broke off the great tree
swam away into the waters as snakes and fish.
Birds' nests paddled away as sea turtles. Leaves
of the tree were chased by the wind and changed
into a thousand crabs skittering along the sandy
shores. And the sound of that moment—the
sound of that great crashing tree—was
swallowed forever in that body of
water we still call Sea.

Sibu
let out a
full belly laugh,

"Water! Water!
What is a world
without water?"
He knew that the world
was complete
at last.

Sometimes when Thunder
misses his wife, he calls for Sea
across the waters of blue.

KKKKkiPPpuuUMMm!

When he calls to her, she lifts
a bit of herself up to meet him.
It is then when you can see the two of them
dancing together ... there ... where the
lightning and clouds dance together
among the Cloud Forest trees.

OTHER CHILDREN'S BOOKS
BY SUSAN STRAUSS

COYOTE STORIES FOR CHILDREN: Tales from Native America
Ages 6-10, 50 pages, two-color illustrations, $11.95 hardcover, $7.95 softcover

This collection of American Indian tales about the adventures of Coyote during "the time before the coming of the humans" illustrates the creative and foolish nature of this popular trickster and demonstrates the wisdom and humor of American Indian mythology.

WOLF STORIES: Myths and True-Life Tales from Around the World
Ages 6-10, 50 pages, two-color illustrations, $11.95 hardcover, $7.95 softcover

Unlike "Peter and the Wolf" and "Little Red Riding Hood," *Wolf Stories* introduces readers to the wolf not as a villain but as a wise, resourceful, and intelligent character. Tales from Russia, Norway, Japan, and Native America help children learn about this misunderstood and endangered animal. The true-life anecdotes bear witness to the strength, heroism, and resourcefulness of this legendary animal.

AUDIOCASSETTES
BY SUSAN STRAUSS

THE BIRD'S TALE $9.95
Stories included: "Creation of North America" (Cherokee), "The Bluejay Yarn" (Mark Twain), "The Nightingale and the Dove" (Afghanistan), "The Hundredth Dove" (English), "The Eagle and the Sunbox" (Warm Springs), and "Spearfinger Woman" (Cherokee).

COYOTE GETS A CADILLAC $9.95
Stories included: "A Cricket in Washington D.C.," "Coyote and the Grass People" (Assiniboin), "Crow's Story," "Coyote Goes to the Sky" (Karok), "God, Too, Lives in Northern New Jersey," "Coyote Gets a Cadillac," "Little Red Riding Boots Moves to L.A.," and "Skidi Pawnee Creation Story."

AND FOR KIDS $9.95
Stories included: "A Thief in Chelm" (Yiddish), "Herschel and the Innkeeper" (Yiddish), "Br'er Rabbit and Br'er Snake" (African-American), "The Birch Tree" (Russian), "Five Sparrows" (Japanese), "Creation of Day and Night" (Nez Perce), "Coyote Loses His Song" (Karok), "Coyote and the Medicine Leggings" (Blackfoot), "Coyote and the Pointing One" (Winnebago), and "Coyote and the Salmon Sisters" (Wishram).

WITCHES, QUEENS AND GODDESSES: THE FEMININE MYTHOS $9.95
Stories included: "Persephone" (Greek), "Maruska and Finist the Falcon" (Russian), "Venus and Adonis" (Greek), and "The King of Cats."

TRACKS, TRACKS, TRACKS $9.95
Stories included: "Creation of North America" (D'Angelo), "Coyote Gets His Name" (Okanagon), "Coyote Meets Numozoho" (Paiute), "Coyote and Spider" (Karok), "The Swallowing Monster" (Nez Perce), and "At'At'Ahlia at the Coast" (Wasco).

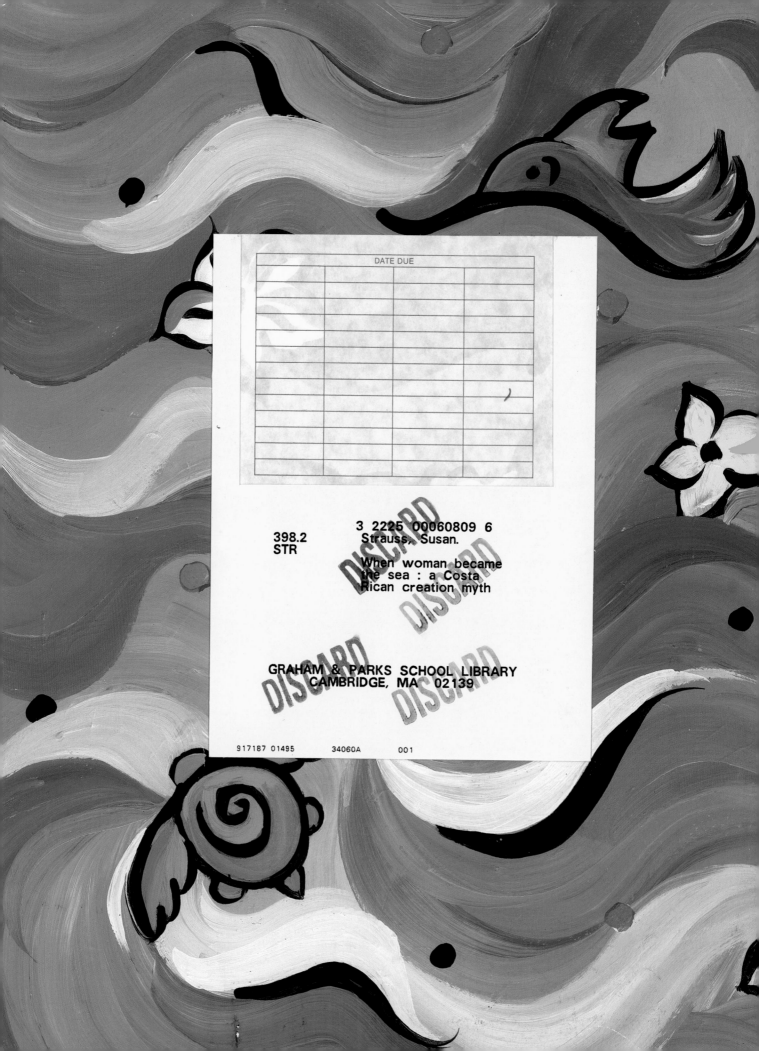